Funny Faces

★ I can name the parts of my face.

Parent: This activity will help build your child's vocabulary. Before your child places the stickers on this page and on the following page, have him or her name each part of the face that is missing. After your child has placed the stickers on the page, have him or her identify the parts of his or her own face. Encourage your child to locate additional facial features such as eyebrows, eyelashes, cheeks, and chin.

More Funny Faces

★ I can name the parts of my face

My Book About Feelings

My happy face, look and see
A birthday party just for me!

1

Parent: This mini-book will help your child learn about his or her feelings. Cut out the sections on pages 3 through 6 and staple them together. If you prefer, you may punch holes in the pages and lace them together. Read the book aloud to your child. Help your child to positively express his or her own feelings by asking questions such as *How would you feel if . . . ? What makes you happy? When do you feel sad?*

My sad face, look and see
My kite stuck high in a tree.

2

My angry face, look and see
My dog playing where he shouldn't be.

3

My proud face, look and see
A special picture made by me.

4

My hurt face, look and see
Where I fell and scraped my knee.

5

My loved face, look and see
My mommy hugging and loving me.

6

Lots of faces, look and see
They are all just part of me!

7

About Me

I have two  eyes.

I have two 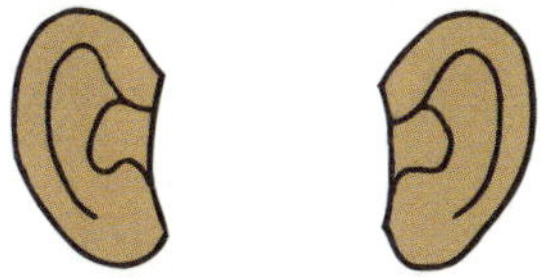 ears.

I have one 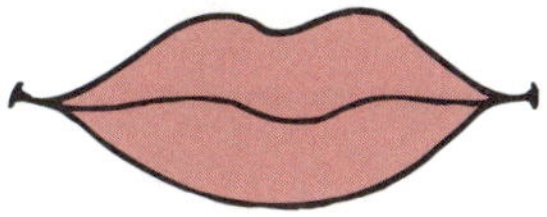 mouth,

One 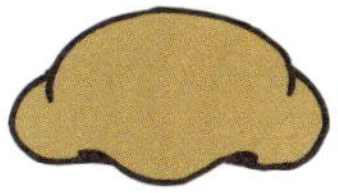 nose.

I have two 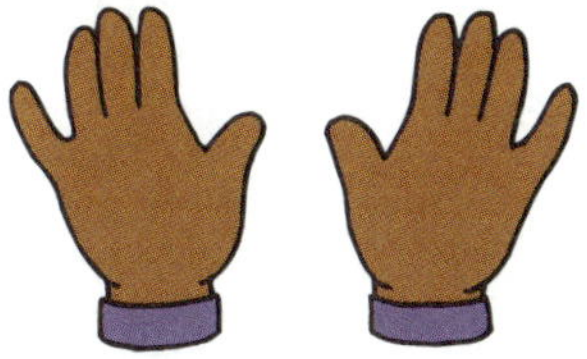 hands.

I have two  feet.

I have 10 wiggling 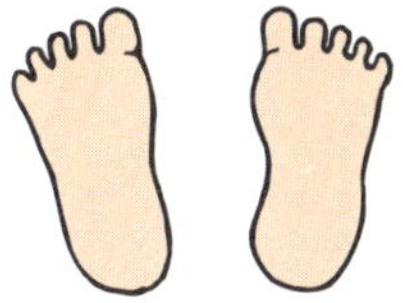 toes!

Parent: Reading pictures is excellent practice for reading words. Read the poem slowly with your child, running your finger along under the words. Stop under each picture for your child to "read" it aloud.

Lots of Balloons

★ I can match things tha
are the same size

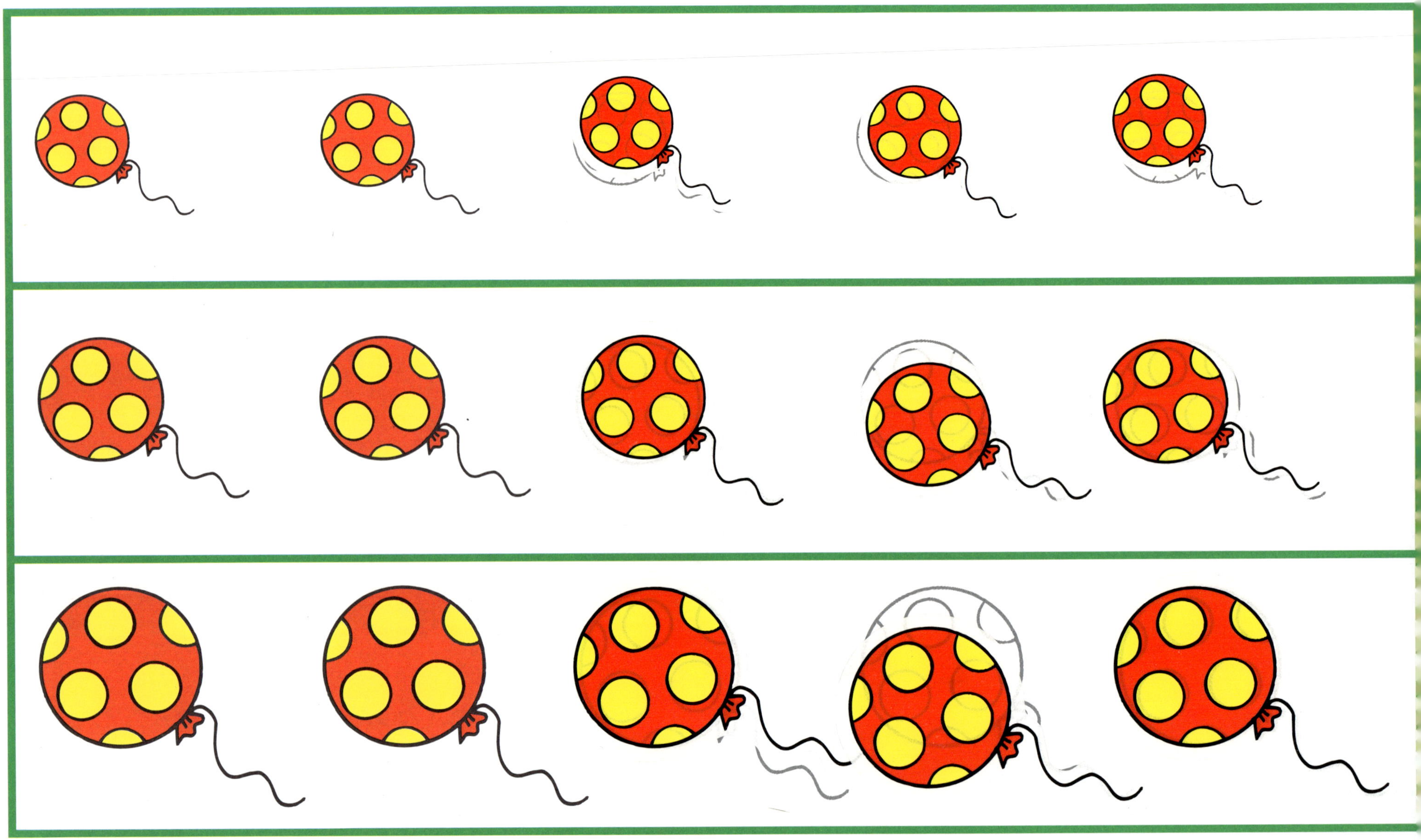

Parent: Making comparisons by size is an important early math skill. There are three sizes of balloon stickers. Have your child match the balloon stickers to the row that shows a balloon that is the same size as the sticker. Activities such as these develop your child's ability to make comparisons.

Big and Little

★ **I can tell the difference between big and little.**

Parent: Making size comparisons helps your child develop visual discrimination skills. Before your child places the stickers on the page, ask him or her questions such as *Where does the little bear sticker go? Who has a big toy truck? Who has a little drum?* Then let your child place the stickers where they belong.

Where Does It Go?

★ I can tell the difference between long and short

Parent: Children at this age may have difficulty with the concept of longer and shorter. Use this activity as an introduction. Before your child puts the stickers on the page, ask him or her questions such as *Where does the long train sticker go? Which toy box has the short snake in it?* Then let your child place the stickers where they belong.

Sticker Pages

Before your child works on a page, cut out the section of stickers for that page.

Page 1

Page 2

Page 8

Page 9

Page 10

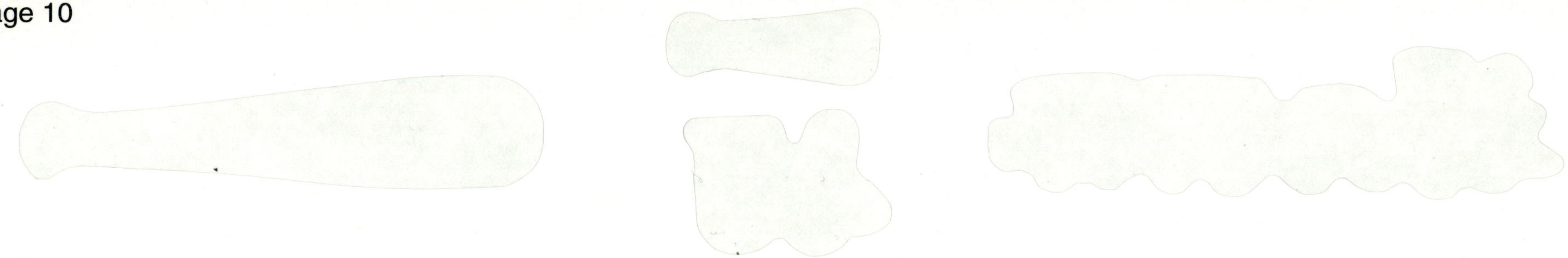

Page 13

Page 14

Pages 16–17

Busy Days and Nights

★ **I can tell what happens first and what happens next.**

Parent: Sequencing activities such as this help your child understand the concept of time. Place the cards faceup. Have your child find two cards that show the same child and tell which card comes *first* and which card comes *next*. Repeat with the other cards.

Bedtime

★ **I can do a maze.**

Help the sleepy child find her way to bed.

Parent: Doing mazes helps to build the small hand muscles your child will need to begin to write. First, have your child trace the path through the maze with a finger. Then have him or her trace the path with a crayon.

What Do You Wear?

★ I can dress the children.

Parent: This activity will help your child develop language skills. Before your child places the stickers on the page, ask him or her questions such as *What do you wear on your feet?* Then let your child place the stickers where they belong.

I Can Help

★ I can put things in groups.

Parent: Activities such as this help your child develop thinking skills. Before your child places the stickers on the page, ask him or her questions such as *What belongs on the shelf?* (books) *What belongs in the box?* (toys) *What belongs in the closet?* (clothes). Then let your child place the stickers where they belong.

I Am Special

★ I can tell about myself

My name is ______________________.

I am __________ years old.

My eyes are ______________________.

My hair is ______________________.

I like ____________________________________

____.

Parent: Talking about himself or herself will help your child develop self-esteem. Help your child attach a photo of himself or herself to the frame. Then ask your child the following questions: *What is your name? How old are you? What color are your eyes? What color is your hair? What do you like?* Give your child help with the answers if he or she needs it. Then record the answers in the blanks for your child.

★ **I can solve riddles.**

My Sticker Book About the Five Senses

You hear me go ding-a-ling. You answer me when I ring.
What am I?

1

You can taste me, cold and sweet. I'm a special treat to eat.
What am I?

2

You can touch my soft warm fur. When you pat me, I will purr.
What am I?

3

Parent: Solving riddles helps your child develop thinking skills. Cut out the sections on pages 16 and 17 and staple or lace the pages together. Read each riddle to your child, and let him or her find the sticker that solves each riddle. Help your child associate each sense with its corresponding body part (for example, smell—nose).

You can smell me as I bake. On
my candles a wish you make.
What am I?

4

You can see me in the sky. I'm
white and fluffy way up high.
What am I?

5

I can smell and taste and touch.
I can hear and see so much.
I can play, and I can do.
What am I?

6

I'm a CHILD, just like YOU!

7

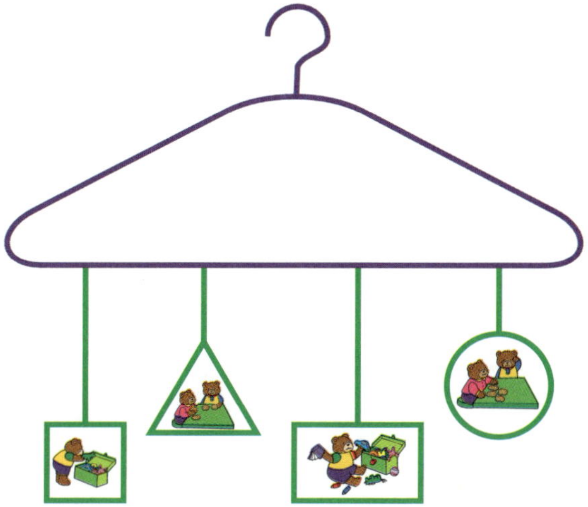

Parent: Asking your child questions can help him or her develop thinking skills. Cut out the shapes from pages 18 and 19. Have your child put the cards in pairs by shape. Talk about each pair with your child. Ask questions such as *What are the bears doing in this picture? Which of the two pictures shows the better way to behave?* When you are done discussing the pairs, have your child separate them into two piles—*Having Good Manners* and *Not Having Good Manners*. Help your child make a manners mobile. Tape the backs of each pair of shapes together so that you have four pieces for the mobile. Punch holes in the shapes and string a different length of yarn through each one. Tie the shapes to the bottom of a clothes hanger. Your child will enjoy displaying the mobile in his or her room where it can spark additional opportunities for discussion.